MIGHTY
JOE
PROMPTER

MIGHTY JOE PROMPTER

(Sequel No. 2 to *Pew Prompters*)
Another Complete Book of Short Scenes
for Sermons, Services, and Special Seasons

by Larry and Annie Enscoe
Authors of *Pew Prompters, Son of Pew Prompter, Traveling Light,*
and other Lillenas drama resources

PUBLISHING COMPANY

KANSAS CITY, MO 64141

To my father
for
finding the road home
and not being afraid to take it.
I love you.

Contents

Preface

We're back. Again.

Mighty Joe Prompter is the third installment of the Pew Prompters series—collections meant to give a church a complete program of monologues, scenes, sketches, and readers theatre scripts to last the whole year.

These are short, easy to stage scripts that utilize small casts. We've written them to be within the scope of any church's resources. There is material here for Christmas, Easter, Thanksgiving, Valentine's Day, Father's Day, and Independence Day. You'll also find sketches for such topics as Christian education, fellowship, family values, and sexual purity.

Since the original *Pew Prompters* was released in 1991, it has been such a pleasure to hear all the stories about how and where these works were performed and what kind of an effect they have had. Keep us posted on how you use our scripts. You can contact us through the Lillenas office.

God bless your time, talent, and hard work.

Larry and Annie Enscoe
Pasadena, California

PART ONE
SCENES FOR SPECIAL DAYS

Don't Be Afraid *(l. to r.):* Larry Enscoe and Drew Meredith.

Photo Credit: Drew Meredith

Don't Be Afraid

A Christmas Pageant

Cast

BOB: *in his 30s or 40s*
RALPH: *in his 30s to 50s*
MYRA: *in her 30s to 50s*
JIM: *in his 30s to 50s*
SHEPHERDS: *in their teens*
SUSAN: *in her 20s to 30s*

Scene

Backstage of a Christmas pageant

Props

Wise men crowns
Shepherds' crooks
Spear
Parchment
Turban
Lantern
Chicken drumstick
Beard
Stuffed sheep
A Christ child

Costumes

Biblical: Angel, Shepherds, Innkeeper, Innkeeper's Wife, Soldier, Mary

Running Time

8 minutes

Notes

The scene takes place backstage, while the Christmas pageant goes on out of sight of the audience.

Also, for those who wish to do so, a real baby can be used for the Baby Jesus.

(In the darkness, a slightly halting version of "O Little Town of Bethlehem." Lights. The backstage of a Christmas pageant. We are behind the background of Bethlehem. Props lie on tables: shepherds' crooks, Oriental crowns, turbans, biblical robes, the manger, etc. At lights, Bob is peeking around the flats out onto the stage. Actually, he's looking at the audience beyond. He's dressed in the white robe of an angel. Bob is one heartbeat shy of total panic.)

VOICE *(out onstage)*: "This is a decree from Caesar Augustus that all the world should be taxed!"

BOB *(to himself)*: "Don't be afraid . . ."

VOICE: "And each should go to his own city and be registered!"

BOB: "I bring you good news of great joy which will be for all people . . ."

(RALPH comes in wearing an innkeeper's costume. He puts on a turban, grabs a lantern.)

BOB: ". . . tonight in the City of David a Savior has been born to you, he is—"

(RALPH taps BOB on the shoulder. BOB jumps.)

BOB: —Christ.

RALPH: Hey, Bob.

BOB: Don't do that!

RALPH: Sorry. How's it look out there?

BOB: It looks packed.

RALPH: I heard not only are the pews filled, but the balcony is too. Frank Sedgewick even set up a video camera so they could put people in the gym to watch. They've never seen so many people come out for a pageant before.

BOB: Ralph.

RALPH: What?

BOB: Shut up.

(Onstage there's a knocking.)

MAN'S VOICE *(onstage)*: Is there anyone there?

RALPH: Bob, you're whiter than your costume. You're not nervous, are you?

BOB: No, I just haven't had any spit in my mouth since eight o'clock this morning.

(A knock onstage)

MAN'S VOICE *(onstage):* Are there any rooms for the night?

RALPH: Bob, it's a Christmas pageant, there's nothing to be afraid of.

BOB: Are there people out there?

RALPH: Tons.

BOB: Are they watching us?

RALPH: All eyes.

BOB: Then there's something to be afraid of.

MAN'S VOICE *(onstage):* ARE THERE ANY ROOMS?

RALPH: That's our cue! Myra!

MYRA *(off):* What?

RALPH: We're on!

(MYRA rushes in dressed as the innkeeper's wife. Eating a KFC drumstick, which she hands to BOB.)

MYRA: Hold this for me, will you, Bob?

RALPH *(to BOB):* Don't be afraid.

(RALPH lifts the lantern as he and MYRA go out onstage.)

RALPH: Who's that knocking on my inn door at this hour?

MYRA: Tell them to go away, Malachi!

(BOB's alone. He looks at the drumstick, wrinkles his nose, and dumps it on the prop table.)

BOB: How can she even think about food at a time like this? *(He paces, wringing his hands.)* Why did I say I'd play the angel? Why? I was happy playing the back end of the donkey all those years. I didn't have any lines. No one saw my face. No one knew it was me in there. I was happy in the donkey suit!

(JIM comes in, wearing a Roman soldier outfit. He pulls off his helmet, puts his spear and "tax decree" parchment on the table.)

JIM: Running smooth this year. No hitches yet.

BOB: Yet.

JIM: Bob, you look terrible. Got the flu or something?

BOB: Yeah . . . yeah, that's it. I'm sick. I can't go out there. I'd infect everybody. I've got cold sweats. Hot flashes. Heart pounding. Stomach churning. Lightheaded.

JIM: You got something, all right.

BOB: Really?

JIM: Yeah. Stage fright.

BOB: Thanks, Jim.

JIM: Bob, what are you afraid of?

BOB: A—Passing out. B—Throwing up. C—Running out of the church screaming. D—Forgetting my lines. E—All of the above.

JIM: Forgetting your lines? Bob, you've been in this pageant for 10 years.

BOB: Playing a donkey!

JIM: Yeah, but you've heard the angel speech 500 million times. Between hearing it in Sunday School and in the pulpit and seeing it in the Christmas pageant, you could rattle off the "Fear not, shepherds" speech under anesthesia.

BOB (*pulling on his costume*): Oh, really. You think you could?

JIM: Sure I could.

BOB: Then take this stupid sheet and do it!

JIM: I can't. (*Grabs a crown and a beard off the table*) I'm playing one of the Wise Men next.

BOB: C'mon, Jim. They're not even in the same scene. You could do the angel part *and* the wise man.

JIM: Bob, relax. You won't forget your lines. And if you puke, scream, or pass out, hey, at least that'd be something for people to talk about for once.

(JIM *goes out.* BOB *paces, then he stops, takes a breath.*)

BOB: OK, Bob, run your lines one more time. (*He starts. He stops. He looks terrified.*) I can't remember my first line. Oh . . . no . . . what's the first line . . . I forgot . . . I'm going to be the first mute angel. A mime in a bedsheet. The shepherds are going to see a bright light, look up, and say, "Behold! In the sky! It's Marcel Marceau!" Oh . . . please . . . God, just get me through this. Just help me say the lines, and I swear I'll never complain about being an usher again. (*Takes a deep breath*) OK, don't panic. Don't panic. Don't be afraid. (*It hits him.*) Don't be afraid! Don't be afraid! That's the first line. (*Rattles fast*) Don'tbeafraidI'mbringingyougoodnewsofgreatjoy—

(*The sound of a halting piano playing "It Came upon the Midnight Clear."*)

BOB: That's the beginning of my scene. I hate that word "scene." I don't want to make a scene.

(SHEPHERDS *come in. They're kids from the youth group in shepherds' robes. One of them is carrying a stuffed sheep. They grab their crooks and get ready to go onstage.*)

SHEPHERD 1: Whoa, Mr. Kendricks, you look bad.

SHEPHERD 2: You're not gonna like yak out there, are you?

BOB: Listen, I've got this great idea. Pretend I've already appeared to you, OK. And you guys can go out onstage talking about how you saw an angel and wasn't it awesome and now you're all going to go to Bethlehem to see the Christ child.

SHEPHERD 1: That's a pretty cool idea.

(SHEPHERDS *nod all around.*)

BOB: So, you'll do it?

SHEPHERD 2: Get out. Mrs. Fingerworthy would have a heart attack at the piano if we did that.

SHEPHERD 1: Maybe we can do it next year.

(SHEPHERDS *go onstage.*)

BOB: No, wait! You don't understand. It won't matter next year! (*Shepherds are gone.*) Because I'm going to die this year. (*Starts to panic*) I can't do it. I can't. I can't. Why do we do these stupid pageants! Everybody knows the story. Everybody's heard it a million times. Why do we keeping doing it year after year after year after—?

(*He turns and sees* SUSAN *standing there. She's dressed as* MARY *and holds the Baby Jesus in her arms. She's crying.*)

BOB: Susan? Are you OK?

SUSAN: He did, didn't He?

BOB: Did what?

SUSAN: Came into this painful, frightening, sad world.

BOB: Yeah, I guess so. Look, Susan, I don't know if I can go out there—

SUSAN: Every year I see this, but now I'm holding Him and I realize, somebody really did hold the Son of God. In her arms. Just like this. God said to us . . . (*as to a baby*) . . . "Shhh, quiet now, I'm here. I'm with you. Don't be afraid."

(*She holds the baby out.* BOB *slowly takes the baby in his arms. He feels the fear draining out of him.*)

SHEPHERD'S VOICE (*onstage*): Look! Do you see what I see? An angel!

ANOTHER SHEPHERD (*onstage*): Where?

SHEPHERD'S VOICE (*onstage*): He's right there!

(*A bright light suddenly comes up on the stage beyond.*)

BOB: Don't be afraid. *(He gives the baby back to* SUSAN. *Then turns and strides on-stage.)* Don't be afraid! I'm bringing you good news of great joy which will be for all people! *(The lights fade, as a single light comes up on* SUSAN, *standing there, holding the Christ child in her arms.)* Today in Bethlehem, a Savior has been born to you! *(Now only a light on* SUSAN *and the Child.)* He is Christ the Lord!

(The light hangs on her a moment, then blackout.)

Bethlehem, Pa.

Christmas Readers Theatre

Cast

MAN
WOMAN

Props

2 stools
2 music stands

Costumes

Modern

Running Time

15 minutes

Notes

"Bethlehem, Pa." is a theatre piece meant to take the gospel Christmas story and place it in a familiar, contemporary context. Joseph is an out-of-work carpenter, the innkeeper a struggling farmer, the shepherds a group of homeless men, and the wise men are banking tycoons. We hope this play will help an audience hang real emotions onto people they are so familiar with—and might not know at all.

Scene One

(Two stools [optional]. Two music stands. "O Little Town of Bethlehem" plays softly. MAN *and* WOMAN *enter and take their seats.)*

WOMAN: Mary felt her water break.

(Pause. The carol fades to silence. Then:)

MAN: They were somewhere on Interstate 22. Somewhere outside Bethlehem. In Pennsylvania. Somewhere. Joseph was straining to see through the frosted window of their dying Chevy Nova. The snowstorm was worse now. Much worse. The squeaking, scraping wipers barely made it back in time to tear the gluey flakes off the windshield. Most of the time he found himself driving blind. Surrounded by darkness. Eyes straining to see down an icy stretch of coal-black road—well, as much of the road as one working headlight could illuminate.

He glanced over at Mary sitting next to him. She was tucked deep into the seat. "You're all right, huh?" he asked for the hundredth time. It was more a prayer than a question.

WOMAN: "Mmm-hmm," Mary answered back. It was all she had the strength to say. Then she closed her eyes again and sank back into the freezing seat. She forced her mind to concentrate on the click-woosh of the wipers. She hoped she was reading all the signs wrong. She hoped the contractions would slow up. Maybe go away. She hoped. But then, she didn't know the first thing about having a baby. This was her first.

MAN: Joseph said: "When we get to Bethlehem, I'll find us a room real fast." Then he wiped the inside of the windshield with the palm of one callused hand. The defroster had conked out. "I mean, there's got to be something there we can afford, huh?"

WOMAN: Something they could afford? Mary almost smiled. They couldn't afford anything. They had no money. No bank account. Worst of all, no credit cards. She had absolutely no idea what they were going to do until Joseph got his first paycheck. She didn't even know how they were going to pay for the baby.

MAN: Joseph was beginning to show the strain. He was normally a reserved man. No wasted gestures. No movement without purpose. But now his face was flushed red, and he anxiously blew on his hands, rubbing them hard on his pant legs. He absently fidgeted with dials and knobs on the dashboard. A dozen times he tried turning on the radio, even though he knew it had been broken for months. He felt like he was going to come out of his skin. He boiled with worry, guilt, and shame. How could he have dragged Mary out here in freezing December? All because he couldn't seem to make things work for them back home.

WOMAN: Mary couldn't find the words to tell Joseph their first baby was fighting to get out. That the child they had waited for all this time was about to push headlong into a waiting world. Well, she *hoped* it was waiting, anyway. What would Joseph do if he knew? Go to pieces in front of her? Fall apart completely? Mary was afraid of losing his strength altogether.

Another contraction hit. It caught her breath. That one was closer. Much closer. That was supposed to mean something. Wasn't it?

20

MAN: "Tired, huh?" he said to her. Then he offered a small smile of sympathy.

WOMAN: She smiled back. "Mmm-hmm," she said for the hundred-and-first time.

Scene Two

WOMAN: Mary and Joseph lived in Nazareth, a small town only about an hour out of Bethlehem. Well, only an hour when it wasn't snowing shovelfuls and their ancient car wasn't stalling out every time Joseph hit the brakes.

MAN: Joseph was an unemployed carpenter who caught the odd nonunion job whenever he could. Mostly piecework and handyman jobs. That was what he was usually called for. Yesterday a friend had called and offered Joseph a short-run job in Bethlehem. He could work through the end of December, maybe into January. When Joseph got the call, he joked with Mary about being a woodworker in Steel Town. But the pay was going to be good. God knew they needed the money.

WOMAN: Another rush of pain shuddered through Mary, and she jolted away. They were creeping into downtown Bethlehem.

MAN: Joseph nursed the car into the parking lot of the first motel he thought they might be able to afford. He looked over at Mary, smiled thinly, and got out.

WOMAN: She was going to have to tell him soon! She dropped her head back and slipped into half-sleep. Somewhere in the cottony distance she could hear Joseph's work boots crunching across the slushy gravel of the parking lot.

MAN: "Just our luck, isn't it, Mary?" he said as he slid into the frozen front seat, slammed the door, and gripped the thin icy ring of a steering wheel.

WOMAN: "What happened?" she said, trying to keep the pain out of her voice.

MAN: "Conventions," he snapped. "Conventions everywhere! Manager said the whole town's booked up solid." Bethlehem had been hit with out-of-towners. The Shriners, several weekend tax seminars, even a group from the Eastern Auctioneers Association was in town for the half-dozen farm foreclosures going on that week. In other words, No Vacancies.

"Maybe there'll be something up in Allentown," he said. He let out a slow sigh and twisted the keys in the ignition. The car groaned, then roared to life. He gunned the motor a few times, then eased the car through the chocolate ice of the parking lot back out onto the Interstate.

WOMAN: Five minutes later, Mary screamed.

MAN: Joseph hit the brakes. The car stalled and fishtailed off the road. "What is it?" he shouted, panic spiking his voice. His heart was punching a hole in his chest. "Did I hit something?"

WOMAN: "Joseph . . ." she said, a thin whisper. "Joseph, I'm so sorry. It's the baby. It's time."

MAN: "No, Mary!" he shouted. His voice froze in his throat. Cold fear bolted through his body. "Why didn't you tell me while we were still in town?"

WOMAN: "I thought I could make it . . ."

MAN: He snapped his hand out and cranked the keys. The car wheezed. It coughed. Then whined into silence. He could hear the quiet rustle of snow on the hood. And Mary's ragged breathing.

WOMAN: "Joseph . . . Joseph, please do something," she whispered. Her voice sounded like it slipped out of thin air.

Scene Three

WOMAN: Walston heard the car squeal off the road. Then the slow moan of a dying engine. He could almost bet on the next sound he was going to hear. And he was right. The sound of footsteps crunching up the walkway to his farmhouse door.

When he first heard the car, he thought it might be the bank men coming early. The letter he'd gotten in the mail two weeks ago said his farm would be gone by the morning of the 25th. That was tomorrow. It said the auctioneers would be there sometime before noon to erase him from the property. And now they may be coming a few hours early to price out the place. Offer their appraisals. Well, Walston wasn't about to lose his last night with his family in the home they'd built, sitting on a land they'd watered with their own sweat.

Then the knock came. Rapid and urgent. Walston stood his shotgun up against the wall. In plain view from the door. Then he cracked the door a little and looked out.

MAN: "Please! Please, you've gotta help us!" Joseph shouted as soon as he saw the sliver of face through the door.

WOMAN: Walston stepped back a ways. This isn't what he expected. Not at all. He had no idea what this man with the burning-red face could want. "Help you?" Walston said. His voice sounded old to himself. "I'm the one needs the help, buddy. You're standin' on a porch I'm gonna lose in the mornin'—"

MAN: "Please! My wife's about to have a baby! She's over in my piece-of-junk car in the snow!"

WOMAN: Walston felt a charge of anger. Please, God, not this. This kind of thing was always happening to him. People taking advantage of his giving nature. Maybe that's what got him where he was now. A loser. A broke loser. He'd always been too soft. No. Enough's enough. He'd seen his wife break down in the cornfield. Heard his children crying in their beds. He did not need Mr. Charity Case standing on his porch. Not now.

"There's no room here," Walston said. "My family's all asleep now, anyways. Everything's taken. Wyncha try Harlin's place. It's five miles or so up the road—"

MAN: Joseph pushed his palms against the screen door. "Don't do this to us! She can't have our baby on the front seat! They'll both freeze!"

WOMAN: "Look, I don't even have a phone to call the doctor!"

MAN: "Doctor?" Joseph barked. "You don't understand. It's too late for a doctor! SHE'S HAVING THE BABY NOW!"

WOMAN: Walston stared at him. "Hold on," he hissed through his teeth. He shut the door, stomped away, cursed under his breath. He knew the motel rooms were probably all taken back in town tonight. Still, he wasn't sure he believed any story about a woman having a baby in a front seat. He'd fallen for one too many sob stories in his life.

He made a decision. Spun on his heel and hiked through the house, collecting items. He came back to the door with a lantern, matches, a sheet, some blankets, and a pocketknife.

"Barn's around back," Walston said, jerking his head off to the left. "That's all I got tonight."

MAN: "A barn," Joseph whispered. He felt tears sting his eyes.

WOMAN: "A barn," Walston shot back. "That's what I said, and that's what I got. Hay's clean. No snow inside. But you gotta be out by tomorrow. Everybody's gotta be out by tomorrow."

(Pause)

WOMAN: Mary, wrapped up firm in one of the blankets, sagged against the barn wall while Joseph kicked aside rocks, old hay, and manure. He worked fast. She watched his breath chug out in blasts of steam. He made a pile of fresh hay. Threw a clean sheet over it. Helped her to lie down. Her head dropped back against the hay as a spasm of pain twisted inside of her. She could hear her own heartbeat in her ears. She could hear Joseph's ragged breathing pick up. Then she heard him whisper a terse prayer as he reached his hands down and slipped them under the baby's emerging head.

"Now the world will see God's face," Mary thought, as she grabbed a handful of straw and pushed with every coil of strength left inside her. She opened her eyes. An old owl sat in the rafters. His huge eyes stared peacefully down at her.

She started to weep.

Scene Four

MAN: Herb and his pals were unemployed mill workers. And one way or another—each had his own story to tell—they ended up on the streets. None of them had much of an education to speak of. None of them knew much but mill work. Except they all knew something about survival. They sat in that class every day.

Herb and the others had been huddling around a heating duct in an alley off Fields Avenue when the blinding light flared up around them.

"Cops!" Herb shouted. Then a flurry of possessions thrown in rusty carts and feet swiveling to retreat—

WOMAN: "Don't be afraid!" a Voice shouted at them.

MAN: The men froze in their tracks. None of them knew why exactly. Then they all turned and squinted into the light.

"Think the cops're tryin' a new approach on us?" Toothless Ernie whispered. "Naw," Herb shook his head. "That don't sound like officer Cruminski to me, Ern. I like this voice." The others chorused an agreement. But Ernie didn't like it. "I'm for makin' a run," he said, giving his cart a shove.

WOMAN: "I'm bringing you good news of great joy!" the Voice called out to them.

MAN: "Good news?" Ernie hissed. "Must mean they got the money to reopen the mission," another voiced croaked.

WOMAN: "Today, in Bethlehem, a Savior has been born to you. He is Christ the Lord. And this is how you will know him. You will find the baby wrapped in sheets and lying in a manger."

MAN: "A manger?" Herb shouted back. "Whaddayou mean? Like a barn or somethin'? You gotta be kiddin'!"

But the light was gone. It took them all a minute to get the spots out of their eyes. Then they looked at each other.

"A Savior born in a barn," Herb said. "What's that sound like to you boys?" "Sounds like my kinda Savior," Toothless Ernie grinned. And he cranked his cart around and was off, sliding sideways in the gray snow.

"Wait, Ern!" Herb shouted. "We got nothin' to bring the Savior!" He turned to the other guys.

"Don't you think we oughta bring *somethin'*?"

Scene Five

WOMAN: An hour before dawn, Walston finally let sleep take him. That was only after he'd paced himself rummy and his pounding heart had decided it'd had enough.

At nine on the nose, he heard a curt knock at the door. He thought it was a dream at first. By the second rap he was on his feet and peeling the door open a crack.

There they stood. Three of them. Immaculately dressed, sleek, polished men. Their faces pink from the freezing air. Behind them, three black Buicks were pinging in the cold. The men smiled, almost in unison. Tiny wisps of frost curled out of their noses. Each of them thrust out official-looking documents, as if they were a pass meant to get them inside.

"You the bank men?" Walston asked, as if he didn't already know.

MAN: The men smiled.

WOMAN: "The ones from the East—"

MAN: "The Eastman Bank," one of them said. They held the documents closer. Foreclosure notices, of course. "Are you Walston Kepper?"

WOMAN: Walston nodded.

MAN: The closest man to the door smiled. He held out his hand. "I'm Mr. Golding. That's Mr. Franken and Mr. Muir."

WOMAN: Walston looked at Golding's hand. His rings caught the low sun and sparkled. "Suppose you wanna take a look around the place . . . since you . . . uh, own it."

MAN: The bank men nodded. And smiled.

WOMAN: Walston's family hid upstairs while he showed the men around the property. Golding, Franken, and Muir never spoke a word—only grunted now and then and waved their foreclosure notices like press passes.

They reached the barn. Walston grabbed the cold handle. "You boys'll be here for the auction at noon, I suppose," he said as he slung the rattling barn door open. He turned to them, waiting for their smile-and-nod routine.

But the men had their mouths dropped open. Faces white. Knuckles red as they clutched the notices.

That's when Walston's knees went weak. He'd forgotten all about the crazy red-faced man and his supposedly pregnant wife. Forgotten he'd given them blankets and supplies. And his barn.

Walston turned to look inside. The man and the woman were staring at him. He felt his breath catch when he noticed the small knot of street people surrounding them. They were all eating doughnuts.

The world went silent. Then Walston heard it. The tiny crackling breaths of a newborn. The child lay there, wrapped in the old sheet he'd given the red-faced man the night before. They had scraped out one of the food troughs and made a crib out of it. Walston's heart burned at the sight of this oddly comforting scene.

MAN: Herb stood up. Pulled his tattered coat around him and stuck out a hand with fingers stained by chocolate glaze. "I'm Herb," he said. "The Little Guy over there. That's baby Jesus." Herb smiled. "Sounds kinda Spanish, don't it?"

WOMAN: Walston and the bank men watched the baby flail in his makeshift crib.

MAN: Finally, Herb cleared his throat. "So, you all come to see the baby like us? An angel told us about 'im last light," Toothless Ernie said through a mouthful of jelly-filled. "That's the gospel truth!" Then Ernie's voice softened. "He's the one we been waitin' for. That's the Savior there. That's Christ the Lord."

WOMAN: Walston hadn't cried the whole time he was losing his home. But now he felt the tears come, turning his eyes into icicles. Another sudden quiet, then the baby coughed a breath and started to cry. He turned his head and opened tiny, red-pinched eyes.

MAN: "And this'll be a sign for you," Toothless Ernie whispered. "You'll find the baby wrapped in a linen cloth and lying in a manger."

"Listen to 'im wail," one of the other men said, adjusting the sheet. "That one's gonna be a preacher for sure. That's a voice that'll get heard." Mary smiled and nodded. The smile was small. And sad.

WOMAN: "That's it!" Walston thought. "Nobody's goin' nowhere today. Not with the Savior here. No one's kicking anybody out into the street. Not if me and my shotgun have anything to say about it."

Walston spun around to have his say with the men from the Eastern Bank. But all that was left of them was the sound of their coats flapping in the wind as they bolted for their Buicks. They left the foreclosure notices lying in the snow. Walston watched the men fishtail out onto the Interstate. "Wise men," he said to himself.

Walston scooped up the notices and came into the breath-warmed barn. He pulled the heavy door closed behind him and walked to this strange circle of street-stained people quietly eating doughnuts and watching a baby cry.

MAN: Joseph looked up at Walston. He grabbed Walston's hand and shook it, noticing how tired the man looked. But now with an undisguised expression of peace in the turmoil. Joseph realized he must look exactly the same way to Walston. "I'm Joseph," he said. "Thank you."

WOMAN: Walston looked at Mary. She had strands of hair stuck to her face, clinging bits of hay. Evidence of a struggle. But she looked vibrant.

The baby suddenly let out a small gasp and shot red, curling fingers into the air. Walston laughed. He felt pieces of his pain slipping out into the air. He dropped to his knees on the cold ground and laid the notices down in front of the child.

"Tell me about these angels," he said.

MAN: Toothless Ernie grinned, tore off half his day-old doughnut and handed it to Walston. Some of the red jelly slipped down his palm.

"See, that's the Savior there," Ernie whispered again.

(The lights fade out.)

Xmas Reduced

An After-Christmas Monologue

Cast

SALESPERSON: *a woman, 20s to 50s*

Scene

A department store

Props

Table
Pushcart
Box
Christmas decorations
Christmas ornaments
Christmas lights
Christmas cards
Wrapping paper
Manger scene
Signs
Felt marker

Costumes

Modern store uniform, apron, name tag

Running Time

5 minutes

(Typical store Muzak playing in the dark. Lights. A SALESPERSON in the Christmas section of a department store a week after the holidays. Stacks of ornaments, gift wrap, cards, Christmas lights, decorations, etc., on the floor. There's an empty sale table. Next to it, a pushcart with a huge box setting on top to pack it all away in. Several signs done in Letra letters: "Christmas Reduced." "Christmas Half Off!" "Items Marked to Sell!" The SALESPERSON picks up the ugliest ornament ever seen on the planet.)

SALESPERSON: I told them this wouldn't sell. No matter how much you marked it down. Look at it. Would you buy this? This thing would give a Christmas tree an anxiety attack.

(She wraps it in paper, drops it in the box. Looks around. Blows out a breath. Then starts packing it all away.)

This kills me. Every year this kills me. Packing up the ornaments, wrapping paper, lights, cards, decorations. I looked at this stuff almost every day since . . . well, since the day after July 4. They're in my memories now. Like decorations I put up in my own house.

(Holds up some gift wrap)

Isn't this beautiful? I bought some of this myself. I used it on a gift to my mother. I gave her a new toaster. A very fancy toaster, I might add. Her toaster went kaput on her a year ago, and she's been burning her toast in the oven ever since.

(She looks around at the stuff.)

Another Christmas gone.

Know what I was just thinking? All this stuff, stuff like this garland or these . . . *(reads the box)* "Multiple Chasing Outdoor-Indoor Lights with Computer Memory" . . . for a short time, this stuff was precious to us. For, maybe, a few short weeks, this stuff took us out of the ordinary. All these bright colors flashed in the corners of our eyes. Lit up dark rooms. Wrapped around beautiful gifts to people we love. Hung on perfect trees we picked out ourselves. They . . . well, they sort of made ordinary rooms magical. You know, rooms we'd gotten tired of. Places we'd taken for granted. We all stood in line to buy all this stuff because we thought it was going to make us happy, right? And it did. For a moment. Now you couldn't sell this stuff if you tried. Not even at half off. Nobody wants to be reminded it's all over.

(Picks up an ornament that says "Peace on Earth")

And all those thoughts about keeping Christmas in your heart all year long? Thoughts that anything could change. That if you just made some kind of movement, things could be different. Better. Happier. Resolved. It's like . . . all those thoughts somehow got marked down 10 minutes after the Rose Parade signed off.

(She picks up a box marked "ALMOST NOTHING!" Opens it, pulls out the packing raffia. Lifts the contents out. It's a crèche scene. She stares at it a moment. Her emotion catches her off guard.)

Look at this. The bright, shining hope. From the first After-Thanksgiving Sale to New Year's Day, this was the bright, shining hope. Staring at us from between jewel-toned Christmas bulbs. Peeking out from behind brilliant packages. All those colors trying to compete with it. We thought to ourselves, "Oh, yeah, this . . . this means something, doesn't it? Behind the packages there. Behind the lowest tree limb. Half-hidden back there. The manger."

(She notices a tag on the crèche box.)

"Almost Nothing."

(She takes the Baby Jesus out of the crèche.)

More like priceless.

(She grabs a sign that says: "HALF OFF." She looks around, then takes a big felt marker, scratches it out and writes something. Then she puts the Baby Jesus on the empty Christmas display table. She puts the newly written sign in front: FREE. PLEASE TAKE. She folds down the flaps of the cardboard box and pushes it offstage on the pushcart. The only thing left is the bare table. And the Baby Jesus. As the lights go to black.)

Tonite's the Nite

A Teen Valentine's Day Scene

Cast

LUKE: *around 17*
LAUREN: *around 17*

Scene

A bathroom
A bench

Props

Table
Brushes
Hair products
Sure deodorant
Makeup
Mouthwash
Bench (or chairs)

Costumes

Modern

Running Time

5 minutes

Notes

Here's a sketch that takes a positive look at teens in love.

Scene One

(LUKE *stands at table with a brush, hair gel, razor, Sure deodorant, mouthwash, etc.* LAUREN *stands at a table with makeup, hair spray, brushes. They both talk to their "mirrors."* LUKE *is flossing.* LAUREN *is popping a zit.*)

LUKE: Dude, it's easy. It's cake. People do it all the time. People who don't even know what they're doing do it. And I most absolutely know what I'm doing. So, dude. I repeat myself. It's cake.

LAUREN: I'll let him go first. Wait a minute, why should he make the first move? Why can't I? I feel the same way he does, don't I? *Does* he feel the same way I do? I don't know. Does he know? Do I know? Does anybody know? How does anybody know? And if they do know, how do I know they know? You know?

LUKE *(dabbing on zit cream):* What if she just says no? You'll look like a full-on idiot.

LAUREN: What if I jump right in, and he sits there looking at me like, "What is up with *you?*"

LUKE: I never thought . . . *(realizes)* she might say no. Wait a minute, when you make the move, isn't the other person supposed to go with it? Come back with the right response? Isn't that just like being, I don't know, courteous or something? Like etiquette?

LAUREN: This is getting way too complicated. Why can't I just go with what I feel?

LUKE: I'm sure. I'm sweating like a pigdog. Already. *(Starts rubbing deodorant under his shirt)* Why am I so nervous? This is something everybody does. My parents did this. I think. Well, they had to, right? I mean, I'm here.

LAUREN *(putting in gel):* OK, you're getting yourself all tweaked for totally no reason. You know him. You've been dating him for six months. He's treated you great. You haven't spazzed out on him. This is natural. This is the way it should be. This is what happens next.

LUKE *(putting in gel):* In life, you gotta take chances. It's the only way you get anywhere. And if we're gonna get anywhere, this is what we gotta do. *(His hair is sticking up.)* But you are not doing it looking like Don King.

LAUREN *(combing her hair):* I trust him. I care about him. I can be myself around him. I mean, we fight and all. But we never, like, get into calling each other names and slamming the phone down like most of my friends do. He never gets all bent if I don't wanna do what he wants to do. Is that how you know it's right?

LUKE *(combing his hair):* I think about her all the time. Well, I don't sit there all spaced trying to figure out what she's thinking about me or if she's thinking about me or if . . . she's thinking about somebody else. It's not like that. When something great happens, I'm like, "I wish she coulda seen that. She woulda loved that."

LAUREN: I wanna be with him all the time. But I'm not freaked out if we can't be together. I'm not like "What's he doing when I'm not around?"

LUKE: She's the one. I know it.

LAUREN: Who'm I kidding? I already know this answer.

LUKE: Absolutely. So, tonight's the night. If I can keep from having a heart attack.

LAUREN: Tonight, if he starts first, I'm gonna be right there. If he asks me, I'm gonna say yes. Or maybe I'll ask him first. 'Cause tonight is definitely the night.

(Blackout)

Scene Two

(The lights come back up. LAUREN and LUKE are sitting on a bench. Both look extremely nervous.)

LUKE: You look great.

LAUREN: I didn't really do anything.

LUKE: You didn't?

LAUREN: I spent . . . OK, I spent about an hour. Or two. I wanted to look great.

LUKE: Well, you do.

LAUREN: So do you.

LUKE: Well, I didn't do anything that . . . took more than about an hour. Or two.

(Tense pause)

LUKE: I . . .

LAUREN: Yes!

LUKE: You do?

LAUREN: Wait . . . I think so. Well, what did you just say?

LUKE: I didn't say anything.

LAUREN: Well, then no. I mean maybe. I mean, what were you gonna say?

LUKE: I . . . I . . .

LAUREN: Ear, nose, and throat.

LUKE: What?

LAUREN: I was trying to be funny.

LUKE: Oh, I get it. You're a crack-up. I love your sense of humor. I love you.

35

(Now it's out there, hanging in the air.)

LAUREN: You do?

LUKE: Yes. I do. Do you love me?

LAUREN: Yes.

(They sit there a moment. Then both let out the breaths they've been holding.)

LUKE: I can't believe I just did it—I mean, we just did it. We said we love each other. *(He grins.)* I wanna say it again: I love you. Do you love—?

LAUREN: Yes!

(They laugh.)

LAUREN: I knew if you asked me, I was going to say yes.

LUKE: You knew that?

LAUREN: I knew it.

LUKE: I don't know why I was so freaked out. That was easy. That was cake.

LAUREN *(grinning):* Wedding cake?

LUKE: Well . . . let's just work with the love thing for a while.

LAUREN: Oh . . . OK.

LUKE: I mean, I want to figure it out first.

LAUREN: You want to figure out love?

LUKE: Well, I'm kinda new to the whole thing. I've never loved anyone before.

(She takes his hand.)

LAUREN: Neither have I.

(They smile. The lights go to black.)

Table for 13

A Maundy Thursday Duet
(based on Luke 22:1-37)

Cast

HOSTESS: *in her 30s to 50s*
WAITRESS: *in her teens to 20s*

Scene

A restaurant

Props

Hostess's podium
Serving tray
Dishware
Pitcher
Glasses
Menus

Costumes

Modern

Running Time

8 minutes

Notes

This is a scene about forgiveness, since that is what the Lenten season is all about: Penitence and Restoration. "Table for 13" is contemporized Scripture that works itself out on the edges of the Last Supper.

(The sound of a busy restaurant. Lights. HOSTESS at her podium. She's the very paragon of calm and control. She smiles at the "guests" waiting to be seated.)

HOSTESS: Please forgive the delay. I'm sure it will just be a few more minutes, folks. We're awfully busy tonight. You know, the holidays.

(A harried WAITRESS walks by with a tray full of food. HOSTESS sees her.)

HOSTESS: Oh, Rhoda.

WAITRESS: Wait, I've got these lamb kabobs to deliver to section 9.

(WAITRESS goes out. HOSTESS smiles at the "guests.")

HOSTESS: Sorry. I know it will just be a few minutes more, folks.

(WAITRESS breezes back in.)

WAITRESS: What do you want?

HOSTESS: Listen, I know we're busy, but we've had a last-minute addition.

WAITRESS: We stop serving in 10 minutes!

HOSTESS: Yes, I know we stop serving in 10 minutes, but this is a big party—people who are important to me—and they really wanted to have a meal together, so I put them upstairs.

WAITRESS: Big party? How big?

HOSTESS: Thirteen.

WAITRESS: Thirteen!

HOSTESS: Yes. I put them upstairs.

WAITRESS: I'm going to have to go all the way upstairs?

HOSTESS: The upper rooms are the only private spaces open, Rhoda.

(WAITRESS sighs.)

WAITRESS: Which room?

HOSTESS: The big room. The one with the window. I sat them all at the big table by the big window.

WAITRESS: Big whoop.

HOSTESS: Rhoda . . .

WAITRESS: There'd better be a big tip.

(WAITRESS goes out. HOSTESS smiles at those still waiting.)

HOSTESS: Should be any minute now, I'm sure. The holidays! Is it me, or are there more people than usual in the city this year? People just seem to be ready for something to happen.

(WAITRESS *comes in with a pitcher of water and glasses.*)

WAITRESS: Who sat them like that?

HOSTESS: Like what?

WAITRESS: All along one side of the table. They're all bunched in along one side of the table.

HOSTESS: I cannot help how our guests want to arrange themselves at the table.

(HOSTESS *goes back to her guest list.* WAITRESS *still stands there.*)

HOSTESS: Yes, Rhoda?

WAITRESS: Why didn't you tell me it was Him?

HOSTESS: We serve everyone here, dear.

WAITRESS: I didn't know I was going to be serving Him.

HOSTESS: Do you have a problem with that?

WAITRESS: He makes me a little nervous. I feel like He . . . sees me. Knows me.

HOSTESS: Knows you, what do you mean "knows you"? You mean you've met Him before?

WAITRESS: No. Knows me . . . like . . . what I've done. Like the time I—

HOSTESS: Rhoda, I don't think our guests want to hear about your checkered past before they eat, hmm?

WAITRESS (*to herself*): Just because you're perfect.

HOSTESS: What was that?

WAITRESS: Nothing.

HOSTESS: Rhoda, would you mind going upstairs and taking their order?

WAITRESS: All they want is water.

HOSTESS: OK, bring them water. Let's not keep the customers waiting.

(WAITRESS *hesitates, then goes upstairs.* HOSTESS *turns to the "guests" waiting.*)

HOSTESS: It's just been a madhouse in here today. With the holidays coming up. People ordering our special pies and so forth. Would any of you like to sit at the lunch counter? No, of course not. Excuse me? Why did I seat that big party upstairs and not you? Well . . . they needed a place to be alone. I'm sorry, what's that? Am I a secret admirer—yes, I guess that's what you'd call me. I gave Him the room because He looked tired. And sad. Unlike you folks . . . who look tired and . . . mad.

(WAITRESS *comes in, agitated. She's got a tray of bread and a wine decanter. She pulls the* HOSTESS *aside.*)

WAITRESS: He's washing their feet.

HOSTESS: Excuse me?

WAITRESS: He's up there on His hands and knees with a towel and the water I gave them, and He's washing all of their feet.

HOSTESS: Well. I'm glad I gave them a private room.

(WAITRESS *doesn't move.*)

HOSTESS: Anything else?

WAITRESS: Something strange is happening.

HOSTESS: Ours is not to wonder why, hmm? Did they order any food yet?

WAITRESS: Bread and some of the house wine.

HOSTESS: Let's not keep them waiting. (HOSTESS *gives* WAITRESS *a little push. She goes off.* HOSTESS *smiles at the guests. She takes two menus.*) All right, Nicodemus party of two, I can seat you now. This way.

(*She leads her guests off. A moment later,* WAITRESS *comes racing in, dragging* HOSTESS *by the shirtsleeve.*)

WAITRESS: Now something really strange is going on.

HOSTESS: Yes, something strange is going on. You keep coming in here instead of working your tables.

WAITRESS: I came up the stairs, I could hear some of the guys with Him asking something like, "Me? Is it me?" and I peeked in and they were all drinking from one glass. I brought enough glasses for everyone, but they were sharing the same glass. Then He said something to one of them, I don't know what, but he ran out of the room and down the stairs and out into the night.

HOSTESS: Maybe he had an appointment.

WAITRESS: His eyes were all on fire. He looked pretty scary.

HOSTESS: Well, now you have a smaller table, so you should be able to handle it all the better.

WAITRESS: You know what they say about Him, don't you?

HOSTESS: What? That He does party tricks with water and wine?

WAITRESS: That He's in trouble.

HOSTESS: In trouble?

WAITRESS: He said too many things that people don't like and He's gotten himself in trouble. And He won't say He's sorry for any of it. They say He might not be long for this world.

(HOSTESS *stares at her.)*

HOSTESS: Who told you this?

WAITRESS: I heard it.

HOSTESS: Seat the Caiaphas party.

WAITRESS: What?

HOSTESS: The Caiaphas party right there. Seat them in section 15. I'll be back in a moment.

(HOSTESS *goes out.* WAITRESS *takes menus and smiles at the "guests.")*

WAITRESS: Caiaphas party? I can seat you now.

(WAITRESS *leads the "guests" out. A moment later,* HOSTESS *comes back in.* WAITRESS *comes in on her heels.)*

WAITRESS: Look, I've been thinking. Maybe I could handle hostessing for a while and you could work the upstairs room.

HOSTESS: It doesn't matter.

WAITRESS: Really?

HOSTESS: They're gone.

WAITRESS: Gone?

HOSTESS: I was hoping to talk to Him before they left.

WAITRESS: Why? You know Him?

HOSTESS: Yes.

WAITRESS: How?

HOSTESS: A couple of years ago . . . He helped me out of a very difficult situation.

WAITRESS: Difficult situation?

HOSTESS: Do you think you're the only one with a checkered past around here?

WAITRESS: You're kidding? You?

HOSTESS: I was in trouble. I was seeing a married man.

WAITRESS: Seeing?

HOSTESS: I think you get the picture.

41

WAITRESS: *I* get that picture, I want to know how *He* fits into the picture.

HOSTESS: Let's say He said the words I needed to hear. Showed me the error of my ways. I'd be dead if it weren't for Him.

WAITRESS: You just don't seem like the type.

HOSTESS: What type?

WAITRESS: The type to . . . you know, sin.

HOSTESS: Takes all types to sin, Rhoda. Fortunately, forgiveness takes all types, too, hmm? *(A beat)* Rhoda?

WAITRESS: Hmmm?

HOSTESS: Don't you have tables?

WAITRESS: Sorry!

(HOSTESS *looks at her "guests.")*

HOSTESS: Just be a minute, folks, and I'll have all you seated.

(The lights go to blackout.)

Stand Well, Mother, Beneath the Cross: Lori Thomley.

Photo Credit: Tony Chilimidos

Stand Well, Mother, Beneath the Cross

A Good Friday Scene
(based on a medieval English song)

Cast

MARY: *in her 30s to 50s*
JOHN: *in his 20 to 30s*
VOICE OF CHRIST: *any age*

Scene

At the foot of the Cross

Props

None

Costumes

Biblical or modern

Running Time

5 minutes

Notes

"Stand Well, Mother" is based on a medieval song about a dialogue between Mary and Jesus as He stands dying. It's about the pain a mother feels watching her son die, and about the love Christ had for His mother.

This is performed in a traditional and classical style.

(MARY *stands before the cross, facing us.* JOHN *stands to one side of her.* VOICE OF CHRIST, *which can be a man or a woman, stands on the other side. The cross can be onstage, its back to us. Or it can be imagined.* MARY *watches a long moment, then starts to buckle.* JOHN *takes her arm.)*

MARY: Look at my Son!

VOICE OF CHRIST: Look at my mother! She is standing here. Still standing. Still.

JOHN: Mary . . . ?

VOICE OF CHRIST: Look at me, Mother. Behold your Son with a glad spirit.

MARY: How can I stand here in happiness? I can see Your feet. I can see Your hands nailed hard into hardwood. I can stand here only in tears.

VOICE OF CHRIST: Don't cry. This is the pain I suffer for mankind's sake. For My own guilt, I do not suffer.

MARY: *I* suffer! I feel Your death pangs. Simeon's promised sword tears at the bottom of my heart.

VOICE OF CHRIST: Have mercy on Me, Mother. Don't cry the bloody tears that hurt me more than these nails.

MARY: How can I stop myself? I see rivers of blood run out of Your heart and stain my feet. I see Your body beaten. Your head, Your hand, Your feet pierced through. Is it any wonder that I am weeping?

VOICE OF CHRIST: Mother, I suffer this death for Your sake.

MARY: Do not blame me, Son. It is my nature that I show sorrow for You.

VOICE OF CHRIST: Let me die so I may raise humanity out of hell.

MARY: Your torture tortures me. I am dying by Your wounds. Why was I not allowed to die before You? A son should not die before his mother!

VOICE OF CHRIST: Mother, now you know the pain of those who have lost children.

MARY: The pain of every Bethlehem child whose eyes went dead in his mother's arms.

(MARY *buckles.* JOHN *catches her again.)*

JOHN: Mary?

VOICE OF CHRIST: Mother, look at your son.

(MARY *looks at* JOHN.)

MARY: Son, look at your mother.

(JOHN *nods.)*

VOICE OF CHRIST: Mother, I can stay no longer.

MARY: O God! Was ever a death so dark? Was ever a death so bloody?

VOICE OF CHRIST: IT IS FINISHED! Father . . . into Your hands I commend My spirit.

(JOHN *bows his head.* MARY *stares up into her son's "face.")*

MARY: Take Him, Father. He is Yours. He always was.

(There is a growl of thunder. MARY *continues to stare up into the "face" of her Son, as the lights go to blackout.)*

So Dead

An Easter Scene

Cast

KEVIN: *he's 16 or so*
CARTER: *younger than Kevin (can be played by a boy)*
DAD: *in his 30s to 50s*

Scene

A kitchen

Props

Kitchen door
Table
Chairs
Aspirin
Rolaids
Alka Seltzer
Glass
Big slippers
Tool kit
Shovel
Mud

Costumes

Modern

Running Time

8-9 minutes

Notes

The kitchen set can be as abstract or as detailed as you desire.

(Lights. A kitchen. There's a table and chairs. A kitchen door leading outside. It's early. Sunrise is just about to happen. In fact, the sun rises into full morning during the scene. KEVIN, *16, is sitting at the table, head in his hands. His hair is a mess. He's caked in mud. Hung over. In front of him is a bottle of aspirin, Rolaids, and a glass of fizzing Alka Seltzer.)*

KEVIN: I'm dead. I am so dead. The minute Dad comes down those stairs, I say good-bye to this world. And after what I did, there isn't a jury in the world that would convict him. In fact, they'd throw him a party and ask him how he did it and he'd sell the book rights and they'd make a movie about the whole thing— which I won't get a dime from because I will be dead. *(He starts to stand. He gets queasy. He sits back down. Groans. He drinks the Alka Seltzer.)* I can't tell if this stuff is supposed to stop you from throwing up or make you throw up. *(He stops. Listens.)* Somebody's moving upstairs. He's up. I can't believe I'm going out like this. In a kitchen. My last meal an Alka Seltzer.

(Someone comes in from the stairs. A figure in a bathrobe and big slippers. It's CARTER, *the little sister. She comes up behind* KEVIN.)*

CARTER *(with Dad's voice):* Son?

*(*KEVIN *bolts out of his chair.)*

KEVIN: Dad, let me explain!

(He sees it's CARTER. CARTER *falls into a fit of laughter.)*

KEVIN: I would kill you, but since I'm about to die, I will spare your miserable, disgusting little life. Dad should have one offspring left.

CARTER *(again with Dad's voice):* Son?

(And she breaks into another gale of hyena laughter.)

KEVIN: On second thought, now death doesn't seem so bad to me. It will save me from having to watch the irritating teenage slime you'll turn into when the hormones finally hit. And then the sniveling little adult you'll surely become. And then I won't have to see the sniveling, whiny husband you'll bring around here. And I won't have to be on this planet when you finally start to breed.

CARTER: You're in trouble.

KEVIN: You have no idea how much.

CARTER: You were out all night.

KEVIN: That's Mickey Mouse stuff.

CARTER: And you've been drinking.

KEVIN: How did you guess?

CARTER: And it's Easter morning.

*(*KEVIN *groans and drops his head in his hands.)*

CARTER: I'm going to enjoy every minute of this.

KEVIN: Well, you might as well enjoy the whole thing. Look out the window.

(CARTER *squints at* KEVIN, *then goes to the window and looks out.*)

CARTER: What happened to the car?

KEVIN: What didn't happen to the car?

CARTER: You drove drunk!

KEVIN: No, I did not. I got wasted and slept over at Grant's house. Then I woke up early this morning and decided to drive the six blocks from Grant's house here. But I yakked on Elm Street and hit a mailbox. I sent it flying onto Mr. Johnson's porch. Then I tried to haul outta there fast, and I sideswiped the Puchalski's Suburban on Maple.

CARTER: You messed up their new Suburban!

KEVIN: The Suburban doesn't have a scratch, but there's very little left of the passenger side of Dad's car. Then I hit four garbage cans, made a wide turn onto our street, jumped the curb, took out four sprinklers, two pink flamingos, three plastic deer, that stupid troll thing Mrs. Nickles has on her lawn, and then the worst thing of all.

CARTER: You hit someone!

KEVIN: Worse. I ripped right through Mrs. Ganelli's lilies.

CARTER (*true horror*): Which lilies?

KEVIN: *Those* lilies.

CARTER: The ones she's been growing all winter just so she can bring them to church on—

KEVIN: Easter.

CARTER: Death is too good for you. I want to see you suffer first.

KEVIN: I've been suffering all morning.

CARTER: The morning hasn't even started yet.

KEVIN: Tell me about it.

CARTER: You are so dead.

KEVIN: Tell me about it.

CARTER: This is gonna be worse than when you put those fake fingers in Mom's Vlasic pickle jar.

KEVIN: This makes that look like a Sunday School project with Popsicle sticks.

CARTER: And you know you deserve it too.

KEVIN: Yeah.

CARTER: Totally.

KEVIN: I know. I totally deserve anything coming to me, OK?

CARTER: This is gonna be good.

KEVIN: Is Dad up yet?

CARTER: How do I know?

KEVIN: Go find out.

CARTER: You find out!

KEVIN: It doesn't matter. He'll awake soon enough. And when he does, Death will visit this house.

CARTER: I'm gonna go wake 'im up!

KEVIN: Carter, wait—

(CARTER's gone. KEVIN drops his head in his hands.)

KEVIN (rehearsing): Dad, I know what I did was wrong. I'll take whatever punishment you dish. (But DAD comes in from the backyard. Behind KEVIN, through the back door. He's got his pants and bathrobe on. He's muddy. And he's carrying a toolbox and shovel. He stops behind KEVIN to listen.) So . . . if you got some Tough Love thing you need to throw on me, I'll take it. After the stupid, dangerous stuff I pulled last night, I'm lucky to be alive anyway.

(CARTER comes running in.)

CARTER: You're safe! He's not home!

(CARTER squeals to a stop at the sight of DAD.)

KEVIN: He's not home? (KEVIN jumps to his feet.) Yes! Maybe I can fix everything like it never happened before he gets . . . (sees DAD) home.

DAD: Hello, Kevin.

(Pause)

KEVIN: Am I dead?

DAD: No, but after seeing the trail of destruction you left all over the neighborhood, you could have been. (KEVIN nods.) I went over to Mr. Johnson's house, and I got the mailbox off his porch. I bolted it back down on the sidewalk.

KEVIN/CARTER (astounded): You what?

DAD: Then I put the garbage cans back, picked up the trash, and I put all the forest animals back on all the lawns. I couldn't find one flamingo and that ugly troll thing. You'll have to pay for those.

KEVIN: OK.

DAD: And then I dug up Mrs. Ganelli's Easter lilies and I got them in water. She has plenty to bring to church this morning.

KEVIN: Oh man . . . Dad, that's . . . I don't know what to say.

CARTER: I do! This is bogus! If I pulled that stuff, you'd kill me!

DAD: That's right. You don't have a license.

KEVIN: What about the car?

DAD: I'll take care of the car.

CARTER: Aw, man!

DAD: Carter, can you go upstairs a minute, please.

CARTER: You're not gonna kill 'im?

DAD: 'Fraid not.

CARTER: Then who wants to sit down here, anyways.

(CARTER goes. DAD sits at the table with KEVIN.)

KEVIN: I can't believe I'm not dead.

DAD: I don't want you dead, Kevin. I don't even want you to get hurt. You understand me? (KEVIN nods.) I love you, Kevin.

KEVIN: I love you, Dad.

DAD: OK, we're settled.

(DAD gets up and puts on his jacket.)

KEVIN: Where are you going now?

DAD: I promised I'd set up chairs at church for the early service.

(DAD starts to go out. KEVIN grabs his jacket.)

KEVIN: Wait! Dad, wait—I'll help you!

(KEVIN runs out. The kitchen is silent. Then CARTER comes down. Looks around the empty room.)

CARTER: Man. There's no justice. He shoulda been dead.

(Blackout)

Across the Miles

A Father's Day Monologue

Cast

JUSTIN: *late teens, early 20s*

Scene

A card store

Props

A card rack

Costumes

Modern

Running Time

5 minutes

(A young man named JUSTIN *is looking at a rack of Father's Day cards. He finds one and pulls it out. Opens it. Reads:)*

JUSTIN: "Dad, on This Special Day,

    Your Loving Son Just Wants to Say,

    Thanks for All Your Love and Care,

    And for All the Times You Were Always There."

*(*JUSTIN *nods at the words. Then he starts to gag.)*

    Who'd they get to write this stuff? Greg Brady? There's gotta be something decent in all this recycled paper and soy ink.

(Grabs another card. Opens. Reads:)

"Father,

For the one who combed my hair,

Taught me to shave, taught me to care,

For the one who took me from boy to man,

And loved me as only a father can."

(He stuffs the card back onto the rack.)

A chick wrote that. I'm telling you, they must get chicks to write all this stuff. A guy would not write that.

(He pulls out a handful of cards.)

You know, this card thing is a serious racket. Mr. Hallmark sure knew how to mess with the male population. He creates this stupid Father's Day gig so he can prey on the vulnerable ones in our society. I mean, he's got half the guys feeling guilty that they don't talk to their fathers more, so they buy a card and send it. And go on not talking to their fathers. And then he's got the other half feeling lousy because they didn't have a father like the one in the card, so they either drop into serious denial, buy the card and send it because it's the kind of dad they really wanted, or they buy it and send it as a way of in-your-facing him about the kind of dad he wasn't.

I don't know why they don't come up with a line of Father's Day cards that deal with what's real, you know? Something like . . .

"Dear Dad,

You Were There, Sometimes You Weren't.

Many Times You Cared.

Because of Me You Lost Your Hair.

Sometimes You Were Fair.

Sometimes You Weren't.

But You Really Tried.

Most of the Time."

> Love,
> Your Son, a.k.a. "The Accident"

I mean, these cards are for dream dads. How many of us get that? Some of us get dream dads. Some of us get nightmare dads. Most of us just get guys who . . . really tried to do their best. Am I right?

(Grabs a card)

Look, here's a card with a fishing rod, golf clubs, and a bucket of dead trout. What's up with that? My dad fished like once. And he never played golf in his whole life. Except the time he took me and my little brother to Scandia's Miniature Golf and he sent a ball through one of the blades on the little windmill on the 8th hole.

Here's an idea. Why don't they have a card with a photo of a kitchen table, a mug of cold coffee, a stack of bills, and a bottle of Rolaids.

That's it. Deal the real.

(Grabs a card)

Wait. OK, here's one. Here's the perfect card. On the front it says "FATHER." And inside, it's blank. I don't want anyone else to tell me how I should feel about my father. What he is or isn't. Only I know that.

And I'm gonna tell him. Myself. Let Mr. Hallmark buy one of these things for *his* dad.

(JUSTIN takes the card and goes. The lights go to blackout.)

Family Fireworks

A July 4 Scene

Cast

Ross: *a guy around 15, no older than 16*
Betsy: *a girl around 12*
Mom Everson: *mother across the street*
Dad Everson: *father across the street*
Boy One: *boy across the street*
Boy Two: *another boy across the street*

Scene

Outside the family house

Props

Chairs
Package of "Rainbow Snakes"

Costumes

Modern

Running Time

5 minutes

Notes

A family values sketch that says the neighbor's parents aren't always better than yours.

(The sound of fireworks. Lights. ROSS *and* BETSY *are leaning against the family car [four chairs]. Both looking glum.* ROSS *is 15 and* BETSY *is 12. Across the street sets another four chairs representing a neighboring family's car.)*

BETSY: Fireworks've started over at Concord High School.

ROSS: Doy. Hence, all the explosions, maybe?

BETSY: We could walk over there.

ROSS: It's 10 miles away, Betsy. We'd get there by dawn's early light.

BETSY: That's pretty funny, Ross.

ROSS: Shut up.

BETSY: Hey, we could watch 'em from the roof!

ROSS: We can't see 'em from the roof. I already tried that two years ago. There's too many other houses in the way.

BETSY: How 'bout if we climbed up on the chimney?

ROSS: Still wouldn't work.

BETSY: How 'bout if we climbed up on the chimney, then put a chair on it, then put a box on that, and then we stood up on the chair on the box on the chimney?

ROSS: Yeah, and we could call ourselves The Flying Bellinis and join the circus too.

BETSY: We could?

ROSS: Face it, Betsy, when the parents said they didn't want to go see the fireworks, the deal was off, OK? They won, we lost. Man, where's the Parent Exchange Program when you need it.

(A beat)

BETSY: I've got some snakes.

ROSS: You what?

*(*BETSY *pulls a box of "Rainbow Snakes" fireworks out of her pocket.)*

BETSY: Snakes. We could light 'em and jump around and go "Ooooo!" "Ahhhh!" Like we were at the fireworks at Concord High.

ROSS: You are such a spaz.

BETSY: Why?

ROSS: Snakes weren't even cool when were like toddlers, OK. Now put 'em away before somebody sees us with 'em.

BETSY *(stuffs the snakes in her pocket):* I'm just trying to help.

ROSS: Well, stop trying. There's nothing to help. The only thing that'll help us is new parents. Maybe we can find working models.

(The Everson family comes out, heading for the car. All smiling, dressed in matching red, white, and blue J. Crew outfits. MOM, DAD, two BOYS. ROSS and BETSY watch them.)

ROSS: Now look at the Eversons.

BETSY: Yeah, look at 'em.

ROSS: They're going to the fireworks as a family.

BETSY: Yeah, look at 'em go.

(MOM and DAD EVERSON open the door for the two lucky little Everson BOYS.)

ROSS: In the great cosmic Match Game in the sky, why didn't we get the Eversons for parents?

BETSY: Yeah, they're the best.

ROSS: I mean, why couldn't we live with them?

(Suddenly, DAD EVERSON wheels on an Everson BOY.)

DAD: Stop whining and get in the car!

BOY ONE: Stop yelling at me!

MOM: You're always yelling at him!

BOY TWO: 'Cuz he's always whining!

MOM *(to BOY TWO)*: Keep your mouth shut, or I'll shut it for you!

DAD: Get in the car!

MOM: Now!

BOYS: We don't wanna go!

DAD/MOM: GET IN THE CAR NOW!

(The EVERSONS jump in the car, yanking their car doors closed.)

DAD: SLAM!

MOM: SLAM!

BOYS: SLAM! SLAM!

(The EVERSONS pick up their chairs behind them and squeal offstage. ROSS and BETSY look at each other.)

BETSY: Whoa.

ROSS: I don't think I wanna live with the Eversons.

BETSY: Wanna go in and ask if Mom and Dad wanna light my snakes?

ROSS: Naw. I've already seen enough fireworks for one night.

BETSY: Yeah.

(They walk offstage. To the sound of fireworks, the lights go to blackout.)

They're in the House *(l. to r.):* Lisa Suth, Jim Suth.

Photo Credit: Jason Brandt

They're in the House

A Family Values Scene for October

Cast

MARVIN: *in his 30s or 40s*
STEPHANIE: *in her teens*
BRAD: *in his teens*
MEGAN: *in her 30s or 40s*

Scene

A front room

Props

An armchair
A TV
A scary video (old-time movie)
Spray-paint can
Screwdriver

Costumes

Modern

Running Time

5 minutes

Notes

A family values sketch that looks at turning off the TV and seeing what's up in your own home.

(Scary noises in the darkness. Doors creaking, a woman screams, groans, etc. Lights. Dim light reveals MARVIN *sitting in front of the TV. The light from the screen is playing on his face. He's watching a scary movie on Halloween night. He covers his face.)*

MARVIN: Oh, that is . . . oh, man, this is so . . . oh. I can't even watch that. Doesn't she know . . . doesn't she know they're in the house. *(Shouts at the TV)* They're in the house! She's an idiot. She doesn't know they're in the house!

*(*STEPHANIE, *his 14-year-old daughter, comes into the room, headed for the front door. She's dressed for a party. And not a party where they're going to serve cake and ice cream.)*

STEPHANIE: Dad, I'm going out.

MARVIN *(doesn't hear her):* The thing is right there, and she doesn't see it. Turn around! Turn around!

STEPHANIE: That movie's stupid. It's old. It's not even scary. Hardly anybody dies.

MARVIN: Look out!

(On TV, a woman screams. MARVIN *covers his eyes.)*

STEPHANIE: Dad, I'm going to a party.

*(*MARVIN *doesn't hear her.)*

STEPHANIE: I'm going to a party with Hemp and his friends.

*(*MARVIN *never turns to look at her.)*

MARVIN: OK.

STEPHANIE: I'll be back late.

MARVIN: Late, right.

STEPHANIE: I'll be home in the morning.

MARVIN: Uh-huh. *(On the TV, another scream.* STEPHANIE *rolls her eyes and goes out.* MARVIN *goes wide-eyed at the screen.)* Man, that is so scary. Right in front of her face and she didn't see it. They don't make movies like this anymore. Good wholesome scary movies. They're all blood and guts now.

(On TV, some kind of ghoul moans. BRAD, *his 16-year-old son, comes in, dressed for Halloween. He's got a spray-paint can in one hand and a screwdriver in the other.)*

BRAD: Yo, dad?

MARVIN *(staring at the screen):* Yeah.

BRAD: Jason and me are going out to make some art.

MARVIN: Yeah.

BRAD: Anybody comes by asking where I was, you say I been up in my room all night?

MARVIN: Yeah.

BRAD: Cool. See ya.

MARVIN: Yeah.

(BRAD *goes out. Screams from the TV.*)

MARVIN: She doesn't hear him? She doesn't know he's in the house. Why are people so stupid in the movies? (*Thunder and lightning from the TV.* MEGAN, *his wife, is suddenly there behind his chair.*) There it is! Right there! It's right behind!

MEGAN: Marvin?

MARVIN: Say something, you idiot! (*He doesn't hear her. He's glued to the screen.*)

MEGAN: Marvin, the kids are gone. We have to talk.

MARVIN: Do something!

MEGAN: Look, our marriage can't go on like this. Or we won't have a marriage.

MARVIN: All you have to do is turn around!

MEGAN: Marvin? You're not listening to me. Marvin? (*She turns and walks off. He never takes his eyes off the screen.*)

MARVIN: Oh, man . . . this is so scary. They just don't make 'em like this anymore.

(*A woman screams. As the lights go to a scary . . . blackout.*)

Stuffed

A Thanksgiving Scene

Cast

MOM: *in her 20s to 40s*
DAD: *in his 20s to 40s*
GRAMMIE: *in her 50s to 60s*
ELIZABETH: *10ish*
THIN KID: *10ish*

Scene

A front room
Outside the front room

Props

Table
Thanksgiving carnage (dishes, glasses, food)
Garbage can

Costumes

Modern

Running Time

5 minutes

Notes

The scene is performed lying on the floor. Use sofas and chairs if you must, but it's not as funny.

(*Lights.* MOM, DAD, GRAMMIE, *and* ELIZABETH *["Little Bits"] are lying on the floor, groaning. At the side, a table covered with Thanksgiving carnage. Downstage is a garbage can. It's outside of the house.*)

MOM: I'm stuffed.

GRAMMIE: Ohhh . . .

ELIZABETH: Gonna pop!

DAD: I don't wanna see food until New Year's.

GRAMMIE: Ohhh . . .

MOM: I'm so sick.

GRAMMIE: Ohhh . . . somebody kill me.

DAD: Why did I eat so much?

MOM: Because we were thankful.

ELIZABETH: I need some Preppy A-bizmole.

DAD: I couldn't eat again if I had to.

GRAMMIE: Stop talkin' about food!

DAD: It was the yams.

GRAMMIE: Lawrence . . .

DAD: It was the third helping of yams that put me over.

GRAMMIE: Lawrence, I'm going to whup your behind if you don't shut up about food.

DAD: Sorry, Mom.

(*Outside the house, a* THIN KID *comes in. He's dressed in old, ill-fitting clothes. He walks by the garbage can. Inside the house,* MOM *leans up on one arm and looks at the table.*)

MOM: Who is going to clean up that mess?

ELIZABETH: I'm too little.

GRAMMIE: When I was your age, Little Bits, I helped clean up the table all the time.

ELIZABETH: Grammie, kids were different a hunnerd years ago.

GRAMMIE: You can bet they were.

(THIN KID *looks around, then pops open the garbage can and looks inside. He digs around.*)

DAD: Let's clean up tomorrow, honey.

MOM: We can't let that food stand out all night. It'll spoil.

GRAMMIE: You'll get ants.

ELIZABETH: Ants? Where?

GRAMMIE: You'll get rodents.

(ELIZABETH *screams.* THIN KID *drops the garbage can lid. He ducks behind the can. Looks around.*)

ELIZABETH: What's a road-dent?

DAD: Mom, don't scare Little Bits with words like that!

GRAMMIE: Well, she's gonna have to learn about rats sometime.

ELIZABETH: Rats? Oh, I like rats. We have 'em at school.

MOM: You have rats at school?

ELIZABETH: In cages.

MOM: Oh.

(THIN KID *comes up to the door. He listens.*)

MOM: Well, I'm not cleaning up all that food, you can be sure of that.

DAD: Just leave it, honey.

MOM: I told you I can't. *(Beat)* Let's dump it.

(THIN KID *reacts with horror.*)

GRAMMIE: I'm with you.

MOM: Unless you think you all might want to have another helping? *(Groans)* It's settled. We'll dump it all.

(THIN KID *can't take it. He knocks on the door.*)

DAD: Now who on earth is that?

MOM: Answer it, honey.

DAD: I can't get up. I'm too stuffed.

(THIN KID *knocks again.*)

GRAMMIE: Well, somebody better answer the door.

MOM: I can't move.

ELIZABETH: Can't budge!

DAD: Why did I eat so much?

MOM: Because we were thankful.

ELIZABETH: No thanks!

(THIN KID *knocks.*)

DAD: Go away! We're stuffed!

MOM: Listen, before we throw all the food away, does anybody want a piece of pumpkin pie?

(*Groans.* THIN KID *knocks. Nobody moves.* THIN KID *keeps knocking, as the lights go to black.*)

PART TWO
SCENES ON CHURCH LIFE

Do Not Erase *(l. to r.):* Eric Loomis, Tyler Loomis, Monica Gunn.

Photo Credit: Drew Meredith

Do Not Erase

A Scene on Christian Education

Cast

Margaret O'Donnell: *in her 50s or 60s*
Dan McNarry: *in his late 20s, early 30s*

Scene

A Sunday School room

Props

Chairs
A blackboard
Eraser
TV
VCR
Folding table
Desk

Costumes

Modern

Running Time

8-9 minutes

Notes

A student returns to tell his Sunday School teacher how much she meant to him. The classroom can be as detailed or as abstract as you would like to make it.

(A Sunday School room. Chairs in a circle, a blackboard with a sign in the corner: Mrs. O'Donnell, Room 101, 8th Grade. A TV and video machine stand on a folding table. There's a small desk with a chair. At lights, MARGARET O'DONNELL is rewinding a video. Then starts erasing words off the blackboard. They say: THE PARABLE OF THE SOWER MATTHEW 13:1-23; WHAT KIND OF DIRT ARE WE? She goes over the words, but they won't erase.)

MRS. O'DONNELL: These old blackboards.

(DAN MCNARRY, a young man in his late 20s or early 30s, comes in, coat over his arm and hands in pockets. He looks around the room and smiles.)

DAN: Hello.

MRS. O'DONNELL *(turning to see him):* Good morning. If you're looking for the young adults class, it's upstairs, room 210.

DAN: Actually, I'm on my way to the nursery.

MRS. O'DONNELL: That's downstairs—

DAN: Two doors down on the right.

MRS. O'DONNELL: Right.

DAN *(after a moment):* Don't you recognize me, Mrs. O'Donnell?

MRS. O'DONNELL *(looking closer):* Wait, you're—

DAN: Dan McNarry.

MRS. O'DONNELL: My goodness. Dan McNarry! I'm sorry, I should have recognized you the minute you walked in the door!

DAN: That's OK, it's been over 15 years. I just figured, I gave you so much trouble back then, you might remember me immediately.

MRS. O'DONNELL: You were no trouble, Dan.

DAN *(smiles, looks around):* This room is a lot smaller than I remember.

MRS. O'DONNELL: Well, you're a lot taller than the room remembers. Sit down.

(DAN looks at the circle of chairs. He picks one and sits.)

DAN: This is my seat. I always sat right here.

(MRS. O'DONNELL sits near him.)

MRS. O'DONNELL: I remember.

DAN: How are you, Mrs. O'Donnell?

MRS. O'DONNELL: Dan, you can call me Margaret now. Or Maggie.

DAN: Oh. All right.

MRS. O'DONNELL: Well, what have you been doing? Where do you live now?

DAN: I live in Seattle. Married. I have a daughter.

MRS. O'DONNELL: That explains the nursery.

DAN: Right. I'm . . . I just came back into town for my mother's funeral.

MRS. O'DONNELL: I heard, Dan. I'm so sorry. Your mother was such a lovely woman. Really. We loved her very much here.

DAN: Thank you. I appreciate you saying that, uh . . . Mag— I can't do it.

MRS. O'DONNELL: Do what?

DAN: I can't call you Maggie. I can't even call you Margaret. I'm going to have to stick with Mrs. O'Donnell.

MRS. O'DONNELL *(laughs):* That's all right.

DAN: I mean, if we were standing in the church lobby or outside, maybe I could call you Margaret. But in here, I have to call you Mrs. O'Donnell.

MRS. O'DONNELL: Does that mean I have to call you Mr. McNarry?

DAN: That's what you used to call me, don't you remember? "Mr. McNarry, would you please stop making that noise with your armpit."

(She laughs.)

MRS. O'DONNELL: Do you have a church in Seattle?

DAN: Yes, my wife and I go to church in Bellevue. We're very happy there. As a matter of fact, I teach Sunday School. High school.

MRS. O'DONNELL: Dan, that's wonderful.

DAN: Yeah. I think so. *(Looks around)* I haven't been back here in so long. This room looks almost the same. Except the TV and the VCR.

MRS. O'DONNELL: I brought that in about 10 years ago.

DAN: No more flannelgraph?

MRS. O'DONNELL: No, I've parked the flannelgraph. I can't move fast enough for the MTV generation.

DAN: You used to use it all the time.

MRS. O'DONNELL: Dan, it was the late '70s. What else was there to use?

DAN *(laughs):* I remember one Sunday morning you were going to play an Evie record and we switched it with a Donna Summer album.

MRS. O'DONNELL: I remember. I couldn't imagine why Evie was singing a song called "Hot Stuff."

DAN: Well, I really shouldn't say "we." I was the one who switched the record. It's such a stupid little thing, but I've regretted doing it all these years.

MRS. O'DONNELL: Well, regret it no longer. We all survived Donna Summer.

DAN: You want to know something else I regret?

MRS. O'DONNELL: Reading *Mad* magazine behind your Ethel Barrett workbook.

DAN: You knew about that?

MRS. O'DONNELL: When I was in eighth grade I hid *Photoplay* behind my giant King James Bible.

DAN: Well, I was going to say that I regret the hard time I always gave you. I used to come in here and try to make you look stupid in front of everyone.

MRS. O'DONNELL: You were 13, Dan.

DAN: Remember when I asked you all those questions about evolution? I'd say things like, "If we didn't evolve out of the sea, then how come we have so much saltwater in us?" Do you remember what you used to say?

(MRS. O'DONNELL *shakes her head.*)

DAN: You said, "I don't know. All I know is Jesus rose from the dead." I used to laugh at you. I called you an idiot for believing in a religion where people got swallowed by whales and donkeys talked and people rose from the dead.

MRS. O'DONNELL: I wouldn't want to tell you the things I said about Mrs. Edison, my Sunday School teacher.

DAN: Well, I came in here to thank you. Even though I laughed in your face, you kept coming back into this room and telling me Jesus rose from the dead. And you know what? I listened, Mrs. O'Donnell. I really did. I went through a lot of hard times after I left here. Some of them I brought on myself. But I could still hear the things you said. Eventually, they got too loud to ignore.

MRS. O'DONNELL: Thank you, Dan.

(DAN *nods. He stands, holds out his hand.* MRS. O'DONNELL *smiles and shakes it.*)

DAN: I better go pick up my little girl

(DAN *starts for the door. He stops.*)

DAN: You know, the other day, one of my high schoolers asked me, "If God controls everything, then how come all these viruses kill people and people get shot and riots happen?"

MRS. O'DONNELL: What did you say?

DAN: I said, "I don't know, all I know is Jesus rose from the dead."

(MRS. O'DONNELL *smiles.*)

MRS. O'DONNELL: You'd better go get your little girl, Mr. McNarry.

DAN: OK, Maggie.

(DAN *smiles and goes.* MRS. O'DONNELL *stands there, as the lights go to blackout.*)

The Multi-Level Spirituality of Sue and Larry

A Scene About Fellowship

Cast

LARRY: *20s to 40s*
SUE: *20s to 40s*
DEVAN: *20s to 40s*
INGRID: *20s to 40s*

Scene

A church foyer

Props

Small table
Guest book
Potted palm
Tract rack
Bibles
Study books
A video

Costumes

Modern

Running Time

8 minutes

Notes

Fellowship with ulterior motives. How many of us have been the victims of this? This scene also adds a satiric look at the church-as-schmooze-ground phenomenon.

(Lights. A church foyer. Small table with a guest book. Potted palm. A standing tract rack. LARRY *and* SUE *enter, carrying Bibles and study workbooks. They talk to each other as if always hoping to be overheard.)*

SUE: That was a great class.

LARRY: Yeah, I just love the way that guy teaches.

SUE: And the way he uses the overhead projector.

LARRY: He's taken it to another level. It's an art form with that guy.

*(*DEVAN *and* INGRID *enter. Shy newcomers to the church. They head for the foyer door.)*

SUE *(whispered):* Larry, it's them.

LARRY: I'm trackin' 'em. Oh, man, they are perfect. I can't believe I didn't notice them in the class before now.

*(*DEVAN *and* INGRID *almost make it to the foyer door.)*

LARRY: Hey, hey, folks!

*(*DEVAN *and* INGRID *freeze. They look around, astonished. A voice from heaven? Then they see* LARRY *and* SUE.*)*

DEVAN: Were you talking to us?

LARRY: Sure were, buddy.

SUE: You looked like you thought God was speaking to you!

INGRID: Well, it's just . . . well, nobody's actually spoken to us here yet.

LARRY: Well, let's remedy that situation right now. I'm Larry.

SUE: I'm Sue.

(They shake hands.)

DEVAN: Devan.

INGRID: Hi, I'm Ingrid.

LARRY: Well, that wasn't so hard, was it?

(They laugh.)

LARRY: Soo . . . what'd you folks think about that class today, huh? Pretty interesting stuff.

DEVAN: Oh, yeah. Very interesting.

INGRID: It sure was.

(*An uncomfortable pause*)

SUE: So, how long have you two been coming to this class. Three . . . four weeks now?

DEVAN: Six.

LARRY: Six weeks.

INGRID: Months.

LARRY / SUE: Oh.

(*Pause*)

SUE (*giggling*): Well, belated welcomes are definitely in order. It's so good to see new faces around here. Just . . . building up the body!

DEVAN / INGRID: Thanks.

(*Pause*)

LARRY: Well, shoot, huh? Let's just break the ice here, shall we? What are you folks up to tonight?

(DEVAN *and* INGRID *look at each other, trying to cover their shock.*)

DEVAN: Uh . . . well, nothing really.

LARRY: Well, how about you and your wife coming by our place tonight for a little fellowship, huh? After the evening service. You know, get to know each other. What do you folks say to that, huh?

INGRID: Sounds great. We've been looking for a church home where we could have some fellowship. We only moved to town . . . well, six months ago now.

SUE: Well, we could have our own little fellowship. I'll make one of my famous triple-chocolate-death cheesecakes.

INGRID: I could bring over some homemade ice cream.

LARRY: I could make some of my killer lemonade.

DEVAN: My dad's got a barn, we could do a play!

(LARRY *and* SUE *look at him.*)

INGRID: Oh, he's just a kidder. You'll find that out soon enough. He's always kidding people.

DEVAN: Guilty as charged.

LARRY: That is so great!

SUE: I love that!

(LARRY *and* SUE *exchange looks.*)

LARRY: Well, tonight sounds great, doesn't it? We can get to know each other. We can . . . you know, talk. Visit. Fellowship. And while you're over, well, I've got something I'm dying to share with the two of you.

INGRID: Really?

SUE: Oh, yes. I think both of you will find it very interesting.

DEVAN: Great. Can you give us a hint?

LARRY: Well, it's . . . you know, it's actually something Sue and I have been looking into recently.

INGRID: Oh?

DEVAN: What is it?

(LARRY *and* SUE *laugh.*)

LARRY: Well, you know . . . it's the craziest thing! Sue and I sort of . . .

SUE: Fell.

LARRY: Right. Fell . . . into this program. I don't know, you might call it a . . . side job, really.

SUE: And you know what, we were able to buy a new car out of the deal.

INGRID: Wow.

SUE: And we hardly put any time into it at all!

(DEVAN *and* INGRID *exchange glances. Their disappointment is evident.*)

DEVAN: I already tried selling vacuum cleaners.

(LARRY *and* SUE *laugh.*)

LARRY (*to* INGRID): You were right about this guy! He's hilarious. Good sense of humor. People like that. Anyway, as I was saying, I thought maybe I could just tell you guys a little bit about it. You know, over homemade ice cream and triple-death-chocolate cheesecake.

SUE: Yes, we like to tell all our friends about it.

DEVAN: I don't mean to be rude, but . . . I thought this was going to be a fellowship.

LARRY: Oh, it will be!

SUE: Fellowship for certain.

LARRY: Yes, this is just something . . . you know, to chat about. We could . . .

SUE: Chat.

LARRY: Right. During the fellowship time. While we're getting to know each other.

INGRID: I . . . don't think we're—

SUE: See, what's so neat about this is . . . well, we could show you how much money you could make on the side for such a little amount of time.

DEVAN: Look, is this—?

LARRY: No.

DEVAN: It's not?

SUE: Well . . . what if it was?

LARRY: Would that be a problem?

DEVAN: Thanks, but I think we'll have to pass on tonight.

INGRID: Thanks for inviting us.

(DEVAN and INGRID start to walk away.)

LARRY: Wait, wait! (Laughs) I know exactly what you two are thinking.

SUE: Exactly.

LARRY: You think this is one of those multi-level, get-rich-quick, get-your-friends-to-push-merchandise kinda things, huh?

DEVAN: It isn't?

LARRY: No!

SUE: Not at all!

LARRY: Nothing like it. See, you just talk to some of your friends.

SUE: This stuff sells itself!

(DEVAN and INGRID walk out. LARRY chases after them, calling.)

LARRY: Look, OK, look! We could just do the cheesecake-ice cream-fellowship thing tonight, and then maybe I could make an appointment and come to see you next week. (Yanking a video out of his coat pocket) You could check out this video on it, and I'll give you call!

(DEVAN and INGRID are gone.)

SUE: Well, just how stuck up can you be?

LARRY: They sure must not have wanted to meet people very bad.

SUE: All their talk about wanting fellowship.

LARRY: Fine with me. They wouldn't've done very well in the business, anyway.

SUE: They're really not the right type.

LARRY: Really.

SUE: It's just they were the only ones left in Sunday School class we haven't talked to already.

LARRY: Really?

SUE: Hey, why don't we transfer over to Al Smatter's video class on Romans? He's got twice as many folks over there.

LARRY: You are brilliant! We'll start next Sunday.

(They walk off.)

LARRY: You know, I just believe it's important we at least offer folks the chance to see some righteous prosperity in their lives.

SUE: Absolutely.

LARRY: 'Cause I sure don't want to get stuck selling this stuff all by myself.

(Blackout)

Be Nice

A Teen Sketch on Christian Anger

Cast

MARK: *in his teens*
STEPHANIE: *in her teens*

Scene

Outside a classroom

Props

None

Costumes

Modern

Running Time

4 minutes

Notes

Sometimes "being nice" is not always the appropriate thing to do. Especially when it means someone continues to treat you badly.

(MARK *and* STEPHANIE *walk in. He's in her face.)*

MARK: Look, I don't like the way you're treating me, so just step off, OK? I tell you I don't wanna do something, and you make like this big deal about it. Like just because we're friends I have to automatically wanna do everything you wanna do! If I don't wanna do something, I'm gonna say, "I don't wanna do it" and that's it. That's enough. I don't want you freakin' out about it and tryin' to make me feel bad. When I make a decision, respect it or reject it. But it's my decision. *(They glare at each other, then:)* How was that?

STEPHANIE: Not bad.

MARK: Really?

STEPHANIE: Yeah. Pretty good. Now the question is: can you say that to *him?*

MARK: Hey, it took me a half hour to come up with that. That's my problem. I always think of stuff to say later. Someone treats me like a dog, I open my mouth and Jell-O comes out. With Cool Whip on it. I'm just too nice, that's all.

STEPHANIE: Nice?

MARK: Yeah, nice. That's my problem. I'm a nice person. I'm not like you.

STEPHANIE: Wow . . . lucky you.

MARK: C'mon, you know what I mean. I can't stand up for myself like you can.

STEPHANIE: You're trying to tell me that standing up for yourself means you're not being "nice"?

MARK: Getting angry is not nice. Being nice is nice. "Come on now, be nice." That's what my mom says whenever I bug out at my spazzy little brother. I wanna be nice. I like being nice. People like nice people. Mean people suck.

STEPHANIE: You do not like being nice.

MARK: Excuse me. I don't mean to contradict you, Stephanie, but I really do like being nice.

STEPHANIE: You do not. If you liked being nice so much, then how come every time somebody puts their Nike treads on your face I have to watch you get all bent and moan about "Why-Do-I-Always-Think-of-Great-Comebacks-Later"? Mark, you got a problem getting angry at the right people, that's not the same thing as being nice.

MARK: I don't see Jesus kicking dust on people's shoes every time they made a bad call on 'im.

STEPHANIE: I think you're reading the "Nice N' Easy" translation.

MARK: The what?

STEPHANIE: Getting angry is not a bad thing. There are things in this world worth getting mad about, you know.

MARK: I know. The environment, world hunger, the $2.50 Ticketmaster charges to process concert tickets—

STEPHANIE: By the way, I didn't tell you this before because I'm trying to help you out, but if you want my honest opinion, I think you're being kind of a priss for not wanting to do what your friend wanted to do.

MARK: Well . . . I'm, you know, I'm not—

STEPHANIE: You're not what? Not a very good friend, that's what you're not.

MARK: Well, I . . . I just didn't think I—

STEPHANIE: Didn't think. That's right, Mark. That's the bottom line. You don't think.

MARK: C'mon, I mean, I might be a little slow sometimes—

STEPHANIE: Slow? You're stupid.

MARK: Hey, wait a minute—

STEPHANIE: You're worthless! Clueless! Spineless! And a royal pain . . .

MARK: *I am not!* Who do you think you are? And what makes you think I even care what your opinion is, anyway—?

(He stops. They look at each other.)

MARK: Was that me?

STEPHANIE: Yeah. Not bad.

(They start to walk out.)

MARK: Thanks, Steph.

STEPHANIE: Sure. Anytime you want me to abuse you, just lemme know.

MARK: That's very nice of ya.

(Blackout)

The Drop-In

A Scene on Family Values

Cast

MIKE: *in his 30s to 40s*
MARTHA: *in her 40s to 60s*
YOUNG MAN: *in his teens*

Scene

An office of a Christian counselor

Props

Desk
Papers, pencils, books
Phone
Laptop
Chairs
Day Runner

Costumes

Modern

Running Time

5-6 minutes

(Lights. An office. A desk with papers, open books. A phone. Two chairs face the desk. MIKE, a Christian counselor, is seated at the desk, writing on a laptop. Obviously working under some stress. Checks his watch.)

MIKE: 3:00 already! I am never going to get this done. (*Picks up the phone, pushes a button*) Martha, what are my appointments this afternoon? I have to get this talk written for the Vowkeepers conference tomorrow. OK, yeah, who is it? Not the Chapmans. Last time they were in here Mrs. Chapman cracked Mr. Chapman on the head with a rock I brought back from the Holy Land. Listen, call them and tell them I can't see 'em until . . . (*checks his watch*) next Tuesday at 3 A.M. Martha, I'm kidding. Tell 'em I can't see them until 4:00. Tell 'em I have a counseling session that ran long. Yes, Martha, I know it's not exactly the truth, but I—Martha, work with me here . . . I'm trying to finish this . . . all right, Martha. Just tell them the truth. Right, I procrastinated on my speech and now I'm out of time. Thank you, Martha.

(*He hangs up. Sighs.*)

Maybe I could find a secretary who's a little less . . . conscientious.

(*He goes back to the laptop. The phone buzzes. He keeps writing. It buzzes again.*)

Please go away . . . (*buzzes again*) . . . I'm not here . . . (*buzzes again*) . . . just let me get this idea . . . (*Buzzes again. He snatches the phone up.*) What . . . is it, Martha? OK, fine. No, put her through. (*A beat*) Hi, honey. I'm fine, just trying to get this stupid talk written for Vowkeepers. What? The Kenworthys tonight? (*Flips open his Day Runner*) Yes, I remember. Well, I'm going to be a little late. What do you mean "What else is new?" I had to move the Chapmans' session till later, and I have a feeling it's going to be some session. Well, tell the Kenworthys I'm helping people. Honey, I'm a Christian counselor, I'm sure they'll buy it. What? What about Danny? Suspended? Again? Is he there? Put him on. You don't know where he is? Well, I didn't have time to talk to him now anyway. I'll talk to him tomorrow. I'll take him to McDonalds. Like the commercial.

(*A knock*)

Gotta go, hon. I think my appointment's here. Uh-huh. Bye.

(MARTHA, *the secretary, sweeps in with a tall stack of messages.*)

MARTHA: Here are your messages. (*Hands him another tall stack*) And here are the ones you need to call back right away.

MIKE (*leafing through them*): Hoo boy, Mrs. Nordling again?

MARTHA: Oh, that's right. Paul Jackson just called and asked if he could get a ride with you to the Men's Prayer Breakfast tomorrow morning.

MIKE: Tomorrow morning? (*Throws open his Day Runner*) Men's Prayer Breakfast. OK, call Jackson and tell him no problem. Then call my wife and cancel my appointment with Danny for McDonalds tomorrow morning. I'll reschedule with Danny for the afternoon—no, I've got Vowkeepers in the afternoon. Just tell her I'll get back to her on it.

MARTHA (*writing*): Cancel appointment with son.

MIKE: Did you get hold of the Chapmans?

MARTHA: Oh, yes. I mean, I got hold of Mrs. Chapman, but she said she couldn't pass the message onto Mr. Chapman because they aren't speaking to each other and she sure wasn't going to be the first one to give in. So I told her to write Mr. Chapman a note.

MIKE: Hoo boy, this is going to be some session. Thanks, Martha. Listen, I cannot be disturbed for the next half hour or so. No exceptions.

MARTHA *(writing as she goes out):* He's . . . not disturbed.

MIKE: Write Mr. Chapman a note. I can't believe people. Most of the problems of the world could be solved if people would just open their mouths and talk to each other.

(He goes back to writing on the laptop. The phone buzzes. He looks at it, amazed.)

MIKE: Has it been a half hour already? *(Picks up the phone)* Martha, I told you—No, I absolutely cannot take a drop-in right now. Well, tell him I'm with some other—Of course you couldn't do that. *(Sighs)* Do you have any idea what it's about? He says it's personal. Ask him if it can wait? They all say that, Martha. He's crying? Is he in some kind of trouble? He did *what?* Hoo boy, this kid's an upstanding citizen, huh? OK, send him in, but let him know I only have a few minutes, will you? Then I want you to buzz me in five minutes and say my next—for Pete's sake, Martha, telling white lies is in your job description! Fine. Send him in.

(He slams the phone down, rubs his face.)

I can't get a break today. How am I supposed to get anything done if people keep dumping their problems on me. OK, I'll get him in, reschedule, get him out.

(A knock)

Come in.

(MIKE throws open his Day Runner as a YOUNG MAN comes into the room.)

I only have a few minutes now, so I'm going to have to reschedule our time. *(He looks up at the YOUNG MAN.)* Danny?

YOUNG MAN: Hi, Dad.

(Blackout)

The Lustbuster

A Commercial on Sexual Purity

Cast

WIFE: *40s to 60s*
HUSBAND: *40s to 60s*
YOUNG LADY: *20s to 30s*
PITCHMAN: *any age*

Scene

A park

Props

A bench
Newspaper
Magazine
Lustbuster box
2 remotes
A receiving "bug"

Costumes

Modern

Running Time

4 minutes

Notes

This is a commercial in the "Warmwater, Illinois" tradition. It's meant as a lighthearted jab at a serious topic.

(*Lights. A* Husband *and* Wife *are sitting on a bench.* Husband *reads a newspaper.* Wife *reads a magazine.* Pitchman *stands off to the side, watching the scene.* Young Lady *walks by.* Husband *looks up, watches her pass.* Wife *looks up and catches him in mid-ogle.*)

Wife: Herbert!

Husband: Oh, come on, Henrietta! You know I look at everybody that walks by!

(*She glares. He looks innocent.* Pitchman *lifts a remote and freezes the scene.*)

Pitchman: Ladies? Now how many times have you heard that one? Or how about this classic?

(Young Lady *walks in from the other direction. She walks by the* Husband *and* Wife. *He looks up, his mouth drops open.*)

Wife: Burnaford!

Husband: Bedelia! You know that young lady isn't even my type!

(Pitchman *remotes the scene to freeze.*)

Pitchman: Or how about this . . . original reply?

(*He remotes the scene on.* Young Lady *walks by.* Wife *catches* Husband *ogling with abandon.*)

Wife: Wellesly!

Husband: Wilhelmena! You know the day I stop looking you'll be in trouble.

(Pitchman *remotes them to freeze.*)

Pitchman: Oh, this is some vintage stuff here. And so convincing, I almost bought it myself. But don't you buy it, ladies. You buy this!

(*Holds up a kit called "THE LUSTBUSTER!" Inside is a remote and small bug device.*)

That's right, it's the all-new, one-and-only, don't-settle-for-any-imitations "Lustbuster!" Ladies, have you had enough of Roman eyes when your husband is Irish? Then this little baby's for you. All you do is attach this teeny bug to hubby when he's passed out on the couch in front of reruns of *Baywatch,* and the remote-controlled Lustbuster goes to work for you immediately.

(Pitchman *unfreezes the scene.* Young Lady *walks by as before.* Husband *looks up, starts to ogle . . .* Wife *whips out the Lustbuster Remote from behind her magazine and punches a button. Sound of a zap!* Husband *howls and jumps to his feet.*)

Husband: B-but Spumonia! She isn't even my type—

Wife: Tell it to the marines, mister!

(*Another shock.* Husband *yelps and drops to the bench.*)

PITCHMAN: Oh, but you say "shock treatment" isn't enough for your little bundle of hormones? Then try our special Sola Scriptura Model. Yes, ladies, not only does this deliver the behavioral modification stimulus, but it . . . encourages the offending party to quote the Bible verse of your choice.

(YOUNG LADY *comes in. Business as before.* WIFE *punches the remote.* HUSBAND *howls and jumps to his feet at attention.*)

HUSBAND: Matthew 5:28! "Anyone who looks at a woman with lust has committed adultery with her already in his heart!"

WIFE: I can't heeear yooou!

(*Another remote punch.* HUSBAND *yelps.*)

HUSBAND: *Matthew 5:28!*

PITCHMAN (*wincing*): Yipes! You know that's gotta hurt. Yes, ladies, the Lustbuster is just the ticket for that . . . incorrigible "boys will be boys" husband of yours.

(WIFE *punches the remote again.* HUSBAND *yelps and jumps to his feet.*)

HUSBAND: But, Muffin! There's no one here!

WIFE: Eyes *front*, mister!

PITCHMAN: Works like a charm. Now you can keep those wandering eyes where they belong—on you.

(*Another shock.* HUSBAND *yipes and spins to look at* WIFE.)

HUSBAND: You look so beautiful today, honey.

WIFE: Why thank you, bunny.

PITCHMAN: So order now, while we still have our special hot weather price of only $99.99. This offer is not available in any store. Just call 1-800-4NO-OGLE. Once again that number is—

(WIFE *punches the remote.*)

HUSBAND: 1-800-4NO-OGLE!

(*Blackout*)

BibleBoy

A Sketch on Christian Cliques

Cast

TEACHER: *in his 30s or 40s*
4 STUDENTS: *in their teens*
NEW KID: *in his or her teens*

Scene

Sunday School room

Props

5 GameBoys
Chairs

Costumes

Modern

Running Time

5 minutes

Notes

Just a short E-sketch on how Christianity can become so inside everyone else is left out.

(Lights. A Sunday School TEACHER *in front of five* STUDENTS *in chairs.)*

TEACHER: OK, people. This week we're going to continue studying about the missionary journeys of Paul. As you all know, Paul was this awesome dude who brought the gospel to people who'd never heard it before. There were no infobahns then. Paul had to go on foot and by boat. And he had a lot of adventures serving the Lord. OK?

(Nods all around. Except for a NEW KID. *He's not sure what's going on.)*

TEACHER: OK! Let's get into our studies. Break out the BibleBoys!

*(*STUDENTS *whip out little computer games that look like GameBoys—only they're Bible-Boys.* STUDENTS *launch into the game with the intensity of screenagers who look like they play computer games for a living. Electronic beeps and tones.* NEW KID *looks around. He doesn't have a BibleBoy.)*

TEACHER: Watch out for Paul's shipwreck! Make sure he jumps from rock to rock. Don't let his feet touch the water or—

STUDENT 1: Aw, man! Paul got munched.

NEW KID: Who's Paul?

STUDENT 2: Clue. He's the guy in the game. Brought the gospel to people who never heard it before.

STUDENT 3: Just play the game, you'll find out.

STUDENT 4: Don't let the snakes on the Island of Malta get you, or you're nuked for morbid!

STUDENT 1: Unless the green snake bites you, then you live! And you get more power.

NEW KID: I can't play. I don't have a BibleBoy.

STUDENT 2: You don't have a BibleBoy?

STUDENT 3: How come you don't have a BibleBoy?

NEW KID: It's my first time here.

STUDENT 3: Then you can't play the game, can you?

TEACHER: No talking, kids. We're studying God's Word.

STUDENT 2: I got bit! I got bit by a red snake!

TEACHER: Quick, grab one of the bouncing Epistles and bonk the snake on the head.

NEW KID *(looking at* STUDENT 1 *playing):* What's an Epistle do?

STUDENT 1: It's a power source, OK. You hit stuff with it, and it vaporizes stuff.

NEW KID: Oh. Whoa, look out for those guys throwin' stones at you.

STUDENT 1: Hey, I'm playin' this, OK?

STUDENT 2: Would you guys shut up, I'm tryin' to concentrate over here.

TEACHER: Cut the chatter, kids.

STUDENT 3: Aw, jailed again? Where's that cool Philippian jailer when you need 'im?

STUDENT 4: John Mark just bailed on me!

STUDENT 1: I'm on the second level! Macedonia, here I come!

TEACHER (*to* STUDENT 1): Raise Eutychus from the dead quick! Before they close the window.

STUDENT 2: Or you get creamed, you lose all your power and your perks, and you go back to Jerusalem and start all over, man.

NEW KID: Who's Eutychus? What's the gospel Paul's supposed to preach?

STUDENT 1: Look, I can't talk to you and play—Aw man, see that? The window closed, Eutychus bit it, and now I'm back in Jerusalem!

NEW KID: Sorry.

TEACHER (*without looking up):* By the way, everyone, this is Kirk. He's new to the class.

STUDENTS (*without looking up):* Hey.

NEW KID: Hey.

TEACHER: Welcome, Kirk. We hope to see you here again.

STUDENT 1: Yeah, when he's got a BibleBoy.

(STUDENTS *laugh.*)

TEACHER: Guess you're kind of lost in this class if you can't play the game, huh, Kirk?

NEW KID: Uh . . . yeah.

(NEW KID *watches everyone play for a moment. Then he stands. No one sees him. Then he leaves. No one notices.*)

STUDENT 1: Whoa! I reached Level 3!

TEACHER: Very good. That means you're going to go with Paul on his visit to heaven. Watch out for the purple angels with the red harps.

STUDENT 4: Man, those things will nuke you for morbid.

(*Blackout*)

On Holy Grounds

A Monologue About Church Ministries

Cast

DICK: *in his 50s to whenever*

Scene

The church patio

Props

Folding table
Coffee urns
Styrofoam cups
Cream
Sugar
Stirring sticks

Costume

Modern

Running Time

5 minutes

Notes

This is a monologue that can be used when talking about volunteers, lay ministry, or greeting programs.

(A coffee-hour folding table. A coffee urn. A smaller one marked DECAF. And even smaller one marked TEA. Styrofoam cups. Sugar, cream, Mocha Mix, stirrers, etc. A trash can stands nearby. DICK comes in carrying a little cup of Equal packets.)

DICK: I better not forget these. Martha Weaver loves the blue stuff in her coffee. None of the pink stuff. I've told her, "Martha, a teaspoon of real sugar only has 16 calories in it. Why don't you splurge this Sunday and have a real cup of coffee?" She just winks and shakes her head and says, "I like the taste of my coffee better with the blue stuff."

I prefer my coffee with natural ingredients. Real coffee, real sugar, real cream. But, it takes all kinds, isn't that right?

(He checks his watch.)

I figure five minutes till the ushers pop those doors open. No, wait. Pastor's talking about his days as a boy in Indiana, so service will run a little long today.

(He checks inside his coffee urn. Takes a big sniff. Smiles. Closes it up.)

My sniffer tells me when the coffee's at its peak. I try and time it to the sermon. This is about three minutes to brewing perfection.

I do make a good cup of coffee, if I do say so myself. I like to consider myself a connoisseur of church coffee. It's nothing fancy, just made with love and skill. These days, coffee's such a big deal. Used to be a cup'a joe is just what you got. Then came Sanka. Then Folger's Crystals and MJB Lite Caf . . . and now you go into a javashop, you've got to know world geography just to order a cup of coffee. Go into that Starfish place and they talk about coffee like it's wine. "Our brew today is Sumatra dark. I think you'll find it has a woody, nutty, fruity, weedy, grassy, leafy taste with high acidity and a long finish." I almost want to ask what year it is. But they'd probably know.

I've been thinking about getting an espresso machine out here. One of those huge jobbers that look like you're running the space shuttle. Then I'll get those tiny little cups with the church's name on them. I read somewhere there's a church in Seattle that does just that. I love it. It takes all kinds, am I right?

(Checks his watch)

Pastor's probably just said, "And finally," so we've got a few more minutes yet.

Now, I don't want you to think I believe making coffee is some kind of ministry. Not like the sermon or singing in the choir. I just think having a place to stand and talk, something hot to drink, people like it. Makes the morning last longer. Face it, we hit the job and the workweek fast enough, don't we? Sunday morning flies by, Sunday evening, few short hours, you're waking up to the Monday morning traffic report. It's nice to stand here and smile over a cup, talk to people you love. And this way, I get to remind them there's a place where people know them.

(He starts pouring cups and setting them out.)

Mark Harper likes his coffee black. His wife likes it with a half a sugar packet and one cream. Their son, Harrison, he's 18 and just started drinking coffee and takes it black and strong, but I can tell he'd rather have it with sugar. Someday he'll figure out he can have his coffee any way he wants it. Kitty Yarrow likes three sugars, two creams, *and* a packet of the blue stuff. Every week I say, "You want some coffee with that dessert?" and she laughs. Carl Cutter wants one sugar and just a bloop of cream. And Marla Cunningham, the sweet old dear, only wants a half a cup of coffee because she doesn't want to be a bother. Then she comes back for the other half. And Randall Merriam doesn't want any coffee. Just wants to shake my hand. His wife is dying. Cancer. He just likes to shake my hand and ask me how I'm doing. He just stands here with me for a few minutes. Then he gets in his car and goes home to be with her.

(Pause. He checks his watch. Looks at the church door.)

Five, four, three, two . . . and the doors are open.

(He starts pouring cups of coffee and setting them out.)

Like I said, I don't want you to think I believe this is a church ministry. Not that important. Just a little thing, really. But I like doing it. I guess it takes all kinds.

(Blackout)